sugar tears

VANSHIKA VASDANI

for
all the gazes that met
mine
even for nothing

contents

preface

i had a dream
my eyes grew roses
at its corners and cried sugars
i wondered how
then i saw
scars bleeding poetry

~sugar tears

moonrise

you said my eyes resided a sun
that could never drown in the sky
it was your world
until you got lost in someone else's
now the sun has drowned
and my eyes reside a moon

i no longer
had to surmise
the cause of lesions
on my body
for you
tried to mend the wounds of mine
with blood in your fingernails
~betrayal

there will be lurid days
when you'll see
ghosts in the daylight
for you can't hide
in the darkness too
because ghosts are ment
to rise from the
lugubrious shadows
                    ~haunting sunlight

when I'm half dead
on the floor screaming about
the infernal abyss
you've put me into,
you slowly bend
towards me and whisper
'it's selflessness'
then i smile and ask you
'what else have you lied to me about?'

you bleed me dry
to alter your diamonds
into rubies
      ~gemmaphile

i was busy being
sweet to people
whose bitterness i carried
                    ~it was too late before
                       i acknowledged

in our story
i was the water
you pulled me out of my home
to the heights of your dreams
you showed me sights that no one could
but when you had
tasted enough of my waters
you sent me back home
crying
        ~rain

i cry tears
in order to quench the fire
of the burning words
in my throat
that turn into ashes
as i swallow them
yet you ask me to have
an empty stomach for your
pride
    ~elegy of the unspoken

i still have the rose
you pulled out of roots
to strengthen mine
it's all dried between the
pages of my poetry
and it sheds its petals
just like my tears for you

~i expected flowers to
stay alive in the grave

you utter lies
until you lose count
do not forget folks
do not forget your lies
as they define your sins
for one must know
the cause of suffering
to ease the torment
perhaps you would never know
how the gravity of
a grain of sand
could attract the whole desert

they ask for love
to stay
just like letting summer
never go away
but they eventually yearn
for winter
believe it or not
it is a process,
seasons change and so does love
so you must remember
we live on earth not heaven
for pain and love
are both served here

                    ~premonition of hurt

and when you leave
for the very last time
you take away your ocean
from my eyes
and leave the traces
of salt on my skin
but i had never looked
prettier as your pyric water
burned my skin
in ember red

       ~water was meant to quench the fire
         not light one

in this cruel world
you can't shove light on anyone
because you can never see the
shadows they create

are you afraid to lose existence from this earth
or afraid to
bear the pain of death?

they say rest in peace
and cry at your death
they don't want you in peace
even after death

       ~irony

i could no longer stay
in your orbit because
the butterflies in your planet
stung me.
so i had to go back
home
to heal

i carry a heart filled
with their helium breaths
as i fly away from their home for
my skin aches
to land on a place
that pertains to me
because i have seen ample
of this world through this flight
to fathom the lore of life

i cry it all to the moon
for its craters were crafted
to make lakes for my tears
but in the starry universe
where it lies
i longed the sun dried my tears
but what a tragedy they
shone instead

we are born so raw
with gleaming eyes
unforced laughter
innocent cries
and infinite love to give
but as we grow in the midst
of the world
and as we meld in the knowledge
of truth
we get covered up with dust
the kind of dust
that neither of the seasons
could wash away
for that is when the
love becomes finite
cries become hollow
laughter becomes contained
and eyes become darker
that is when we grow

that is the thing about growing
you lose petals
long before you bloom

we spent our days
stealing feathers for our butterfly wings
too naive to understand
the beauty of
our own design
                    ~comparison

time.
something that i could never
catch hold of
something that hides
the past in oblivion
something that my
fears are parallel to
                    ~something i'm afraid of

but there was a difference
between
seeing the world
through the heights of the sky
and
feeling the bombs dig into your land
there was a difference between
understanding someone's grief
and feeling it

i sit there in silence
and the voices crash
bruising my soul
a violent hate bleeding
for this isn't silence
it's just an illusion

i am closing my eyes shut
to lay on the blues
wake me up when
i grow out of this predicament
wake me up when
the stars stop flowing from my eyes
and we've reached the shore
                              ~when the melancholy
                              ceases

sunrise

it takes time
doesn't it?
to shred the mud
from my body
that we fought into
and to remove the
stabbed knives from my back
it takes time to
get used to watching
the bruises
                ~the healing

"band aids?" she asks
"i've gotten plenty of them, but i'm not sure if the
bruises on your knees are caused by kneeling for love
or forgiveness because aches like these, my love, can
only be cured by the right aid."

unfortunately
i did not realise that
i was locking myself up
behind the bars that i built
to lose your sight
so i throw the hinges and screws away
and evict you
from being my grief
~i set you free

when i wept
about my riven heart
that i lugged through time
they told me
i was lucky to carry love
in a million pieces
because mediocre hearts
like mine
were scenic as they were
capable of sharing love
to a million
   ~family

stop.
stop pouring little one
do not mourn
do not drown your
paper boats away
in the puddles of obnoxity for
you were meant to
run towards east
behind the streams of sun rays
so blow your paper boats
towards the east and
run,
run with joy spilling
out of your soul
stop pouring little one
before the climate changes
and there are no
blue floors
for your paper boats

it has been a long time
since i've let my fears petrify me
by the way they dance inside me
as i failed to realise
that it was a ballroom
that belonged to myself
and that we were supposed to
waltz together
all this time
so i gather valiance
and embrace them
as they paralyse and slip away
from my hands and feet
and run to the audience seat
where i'd been sitting before
a smirk wears on my lips
as i say
"now watch me dance!"

at times when
the fear creeps in
and the slow pace of my heart
becomes a little too fast
i do not forget to remind myself that
i've danced to this wretched beat before

~party of
fears

i'm like the ends of a flag
weathered threads with distant endings
for these bruises push me to the beginnings

everyone envied
the bohemian scars
that your weapons left
on my body
for i was no longer
afraid of wars
if they left
ineffable

      traces

          on me

              ~fears are traded for bruises

i could see the
sun burning
as if the cold night
was melting with my numbness
the stars hiding
in the warm light
the snow thawing in my eyes
streaming tears
                    ~hope

regret is a wound that can heal

how did i forget
that my skin is a twin
to the soil i walk upon
i will experience every summer breeze
and winter night
i will go through it all
just to come back to every season
with a new ache
however i will still gleam
without letting this ache blemish
my will
as i will be a wounded feral
with handwritten scars of fate
on my skin
that resemble strength

you wanted to move my world
saying that the fields
on it needed
more than a
shake of wind
but don't you know
what storms lead to?
distortion.
of the picturesque
scarlet flowers and rivulets
that had just formed
for how could i enjoy
the wild storm
when i was
longing
for
spring

why did you come searching for me
when you told me to hide

~hide & seek

you sail on my translucent blues
to perceive my
internal beauty
but did you forget?
my allure was hefty
it stayed in the deposits
of my sweet ocean
it was only found
when you dove into
the depth of dead

i love god
because he never left us with
complete darkness
he left us the moon
with its scars on full display
as if the night is a mirror
of our
shattered lives
and all the good parts of it
are scattered away
in the stars

        in
infinite
        pieces
   of
      light

perhaps
in this rush of time
i'm not a roller coaster ride
that could blur the sights
out of your eyes
i'm a giant wheel
that could drift you
to the heights of your emotions
with a pace
that could show you
lifetimes with a
blink of an eye

                    ~city fair

i'm not amongst the multitude
i carry a garden
full of wildflowers
betweeen the cracks
of my barren gold
for the crowds chop
their evergreens from
their fertile flesh
as they languish to
cultivate a counterfeit copy
of my beauty
when they watch me flourish
so don't you dare
call me amongst the multitude

~influence

sometimes i wonder
about the old woman inside me
for she carries many smiles on her wrinkles
and walks like flowing water
she has lived
the nicety of superficial dreams
that stay in my eyes
and perhaps it is not lucid
to embrace a skin so ineffable
but it has always been
scandal to be yourself
so it's up to me to be
the old woman inside me

~manifestation

even after looking at your
reflection everyday
in the mirror you ask people
if you are beautiful
                    ~illusion of beliefs

be the kind of daylight
that makes the
stars disappear
even though they exist

i carry it like a privilege
that not everyone has
not everyone can have
it's all fit
in my body like
art
like gold running in my veins
that the pages mine for
                              ~poetry

aren't we butterflies
we enter a body
grow old and beautiful
and leave a body
to enter another one
                    ~the process

we consume ourselves with the filth of fear as we live. we wait for the world to end to live fully. that is what makes us average. we choose to leave only a few blank pages at the end of our story to experience the thrill of life, unaware of the fact that we hold the power to tranquil our mundane lives into the extraordinary ones whenever we want to

~the last time

i am a foolish floral
i expect not to get plucked
nevertheless if i lose my life
do not torture me with a beautiful vase
until i perish
but gift me with a afterlife
in the coffin of your pages

when i leave the earth
i long for my soul
to watch the sun shine
as my shadows endure
and hear the chaos of the world
without my breath
i long to ask the earth
if my body
has become lighter
in the grave
without the weight of
my soul in it

time takes it all
it peels the skin out of your bones
to birth a new one
it blows away
all the hurt
but it never forgets
to take away all the
timeless moments
from you
it shows no mercy
to both the
devil and the angel
on your shoulder
                    ~balance

for once
i think if it was all
meant to happen
and if all these souls were
ment to meet mine

~everything feels so happened to
my soul

i never knew
that i had cocoons
in my stomach
not until i saw you
and it broke
setting all the butterflies
free through my heart

when you look
at me
with those eyes
everything around us
sets on fire
but don't you know?
you make it look like fireworks
for imagine
how beautiful the sky would be
when i'd call you
mine
        ~state of grace

there's always a way
the rain embraces the soil
and the way they dissolve in themselves
and speak of love
with their voices echoing
in the air
          ~the way nature romanticizes

while the rest
of the world is
busy adoring my petals
i hope you adore
all that i have come here with
i hope you adore my
leaves and stems
and the roots that
feed me
for my existence

will you be my earth
when i pour rain on you?
will you save
your burning roots
with my sorrow?
                    ~when our sadness conflates

how thrilling is it to know
that we know nothing about
the strangers that enter our lives
they enter our cosmos with stars gleaming in their
eyes
but not everyone stays
some wait until sunset
some wait until your days unravel into nights
their shadows emerge with the darkness
yet they dont leave
they hold your hand
and point to the stars in the sky
that once
gleamed in their eyes
                    ~the ones who are
                      stargazing with me

when the blinding lights
get too harsh
do not mistake
the shadows for shade

~lesson 1

when you stand
in the battlefield to
combat your foes
do not neglect the fright
of conflict among your
own army
beware of your pawns
for you might never know
when their white shields
rinse into black
since the only power held
by the vulnerable troops
is to exploit the potent queen

~lesson 2

i am the alchemist
i am not amongst
your selfish companions
who are guided by false maps
towards arid lands
mobilising in search of gold
i am the creator
of the treasure
they will never find
~companionship

there will be times
when reality feels like
a delusion
when you get caught up
in the moments
there will be times
that you would want to hold onto
forever
the ones that you
would want to lure
in the palm of your hands
but darling
we are not surrounded
by walls that could
resonate the good times
we are surrounded by
air
that lets them pass

ugly
        smiles
                are
                        the
                                happiest

can you taste
the vanilla on the
tongue of my life

how could time echo
if the universe is wounded
it could never come back
once it passes through the stars

~celestial secret

we will all die
whether in the drowning sun
or rising waters
we were all meant
to silence the world
so the nature could scream its beauty
through pain
and be ready to bear it all
once again
       ~truth

i was born without wings
but i still flied
                    ~the other birds were jealous of me

one day
i would come with so much brightness
your eyes couldn't meet mine

                              ~sun

dear god
don't you get bored
watching us?
because you already know
what's going to happen next

~reality

they say you experience joy
long before it rolls
on your path,
every vein in your body
tends to sense
the warmth of zest
before it embraces you
and so did i feel the
warmth of your sunlit gazes
meeting the horizon of
my oceanic pages
even before the
evening occurred
~sunset

acknowledgements

firstly, thank you to my dear friend Vidhi Ghodawat. for all your support and insight towards shaping this book and for walking through each line with me, you deserve all the love.

to everyone who helped in big ways and small- thank you.

to all my readers, thank you for holding a piece of my mosaic heart.

and lastly thank you to all those who gave me grief and poetry.

www.ingramcontent.com/pod-product-compliance
Lightning Source LLC
Chambersburg PA
CBHW020501160726
47991CB00007B/2756